By Chad Gillespie Tavares
©Inspire Learning 2022
ISBN 978-1-952414-05-3

100 Hopeful Prayers

Prayers For Myself

1. A Prayer For God's Eternal Love
2. A Prayer For Healing
3. A Prayer To Be Faithful
4. A Prayer For Wisdom
5. A Prayer To Help Me Find My Way
6. A Prayer For Obedience
7. A Prayer For Holy Spirit
8. A Prayer For A Godly Character
9. A Prayer To Find Kind Words
10. A Prayer To Help With Anger
11. A Prayer To Help with Jealousy
12. A Prayer Of Gratitude
13. A Prayer For Difficult Times
14. A Prayer To Love
15. A Prayer For A Good Job Interview
16. A Prayer For My Upcoming Surgery
17. A Prayer To Trust In God
18. A Prayer For My Good Health
19. A Prayer To Feel God's Presence
20. A Prayer For My Broken Heart
21. A Prayer For Perseverance
22. A Prayer For Self Control
23. A Prayer For Feelings of Unworth
24. A Prayer For Healthy Eating
25. A Prayer For Self Doubt

Prayers For My Friends and Family

26. A Prayer To Show Love
27. A Prayer For Concerns About Safety
28. A Prayer For Upcoming Surgery
29. A Prayer For My Pet's Health
30. A Prayer For My Pet's Happiness
31. A Prayer For Those Who Left Us
32. A Prayer For Recovery
33. A Prayer For Those Struggling With Loss
34. A Prayer For Healing
35. A Prayer For Success
36. A Prayer For Divine Guidance
37. A Prayer Of Blessings
38. A Prayer For A Friend Losing Faith
39. A Prayer To Love When It's Hard
40. A Prayer For A Peaceful Home
41. A Prayer For Restoring Relationships
42. A Prayer For Meals
43. A Prayer For Bedtime
44. A Prayer For Our Visitors
45. A Prayer Before Travel
46. A Prayer For Reconciliation
47. A Prayer For A Loving Family
48. A Prayer For A New Family Member
49. A Prayer To Find Gratitude
50. A Prayer To Make Nice

Prayers For My Community

51. A Prayer For Our Community Leaders
52. A Prayer For A Safe Community
53. A Prayer For Our Schools
54. A Prayer For Our Local Businesses
55. A Prayer For Our Healthcare Community
56. A Prayer For Our Local Churches
57. A Prayer For Our Community's Families
58. A Prayer For Our Seniors
59. A Prayer For Artists And Creators
60. A Prayer For Our First Responders
61. A Prayer For Journalists
62. A Prayer For Politicians
63. A Prayer For Local Farmers
64. A Prayer For Mental Well Being
65. A Prayer For Spiritual Growth
66. A Prayer For Happiness, Love, And Joy
67. A Prayer For Community Connection
68. A Prayer During Disaster
69. A Prayer For Our Young Adults
70. A Prayer For the Parents
71. A Prayer For Our Team
72. A Prayer For New Years
73. A Christmas Community Prayer
74. A Prayer For Our Neighbors
75. A Prayer For The Lonely

Prayers For All

76. A Prayer For Good Health For The Ill
77. A Prayer For The Hungry
78. A Prayer For World Peace
79. A Prayer For The Poor And Homeless
80. A Prayer For Kindness To The Earth
81. A Prayer For Kindness and Respect
82. A Prayer For Education
83. A Prayer For Understanding
84. A Prayer To Know God's Love
85. A Pray For Inspiration
86. A Prayer For Connection
87. A Prayer For Winter Safety
88. A Prayer For Those Away From Home
89. Prayer For Those With Dangerous Jobs
90. A Prayer For The Isolated
91. A Prayer For The Disabled
92. A Prayer For the Unborn
93. A Prayer For Broken Families
94. A Prayer For the Dying
95. A Prayer For the Displaced
96. A Prayer For Immigrants
97. A Prayer For the Children
98. A Prayer For the Desperate
99. A Prayer For the Corrupt
100. A Prayer For The Lord's Light

Prayers For Myself

1. A Prayer For God's Eternal Love

I come to you today with a heart full of gratitude for your endless love and mercy. I thank you for your never-ending grace and forgiveness, and for the gift of eternal life through your Son, Jesus.

I pray that I may always feel the depth and power of your love, and that it may be a source of strength and comfort for me in all circumstances. May I always turn to you in times of need, and may I find rest and peace in your loving arms.

I pray that I may grow in my understanding of your love, and that it may shape and guide every aspect of my life. May I be a beacon of your love to those around me, and may I share it generously with all those I encounter.

I pray for the power of your love to transform the world, and for the grace to bring healing and hope to all those who are lost and hurting. May your love be a light in the darkness, and may it shine brightly for all eternity.
In your holy name I pray, Amen.

2. A Prayer For Healing

Dear God,

I come to you today with a heart that is hurting and in need of your healing touch. I know that you are the source of all comfort and healing, and I pray that you would bring your love and peace to my broken heart.

I pray for the strength and courage to face each day, and for the wisdom to navigate my pain and hurt. May I find hope and healing in your love, and may I know that I am not alone in this struggle.

I pray for the people in my life who love and care for me, that they may be a source of support and encouragement as I navigate this difficult time. May they be patient, kind, and understanding as they offer their love and support.

I pray for the power of your love to bring healing and restoration to my broken heart, and for the grace to overcome the challenges I am facing. May I find strength and hope in you, and may I know that you are with me every step of the way.

In your holy name I pray, Amen.

3. A Prayer To Be Faithful

Dear God,

I desire to be faithful in all that I do. I know that faithfulness is a cornerstone of a healthy and fulfilling life, and I pray for your help in cultivating it in my life.

I pray for the wisdom to understand the importance of faithfulness, and for the grace to be reliable and dependable in all that I do. May I have the courage and strength to follow through on my commitments, and may I always seek to be true to my word.

I pray for the power of your love to transform my heart and mind, and for the grace to overcome any negative patterns or habits that may hinder my faithfulness. May I always strive to be honest and trustworthy, and may I seek to bring love and compassion to all those I encounter.

I pray that my life may be a reflection of your love and grace, and that it may bring joy and hope to all those who encounter it. May I always seek to be faithful in all that I do, and may I know the fullness of your love in every moment. In your holy name I pray, Amen.

4. A Prayer For Wisdom

Dear God,

I am seeking your wisdom and guidance. I know that you are the source of all knowledge and understanding, and I pray for your help in navigating the challenges and decisions of life.

I pray for the wisdom to understand your will for my life, and for the grace to follow it faithfully. May I have the courage and strength to seek your guidance in all that I do, and may I find peace and joy in your loving arms.

I pray for the power of your love to transform my heart and mind, and for the grace to overcome any negative patterns or habits that may hinder my growth. May I always strive to be open to your leading and guidance, and may I seek to bring love and compassion to all those I encounter.

I pray that my life may be a reflection of your love and grace, and that it may bring joy and hope to all those who encounter it. May I always seek to grow in wisdom and understanding, and may I know the fullness of your love in every moment. In your holy name I pray, Amen.

5. A Prayer To Help Me Find My Way

Dear God,

I am in need of your guidance. I know that you are the source of all wisdom and direction, and I pray that you would bring your light and guidance to my path.

I pray for the strength and courage to face each day, and for the wisdom to navigate the decisions and challenges that come my way. May I find hope and purpose in your love, and may I know that I am not alone in this journey.

I pray for the people in my life who love and care for me, that they may be a source of support and encouragement as I search for my way. May they be patient, kind, and understanding as they offer their love and support.

I pray for the power of your love to guide and direct my path, and for the grace to overcome the obstacles that may come my way. May I find strength and hope in you, and may I know that you are with me every step of the way.

In your holy name I pray, Amen.

6. A Prayer For Obedience

Dear God,

I am grateful for your constant presence in my life. I thank you for the gift of salvation through your Son, Jesus, and for the opportunity to walk in his footsteps every day.

I pray for the strength and courage to abide by Christ in all that I do, and for the wisdom to follow his example in my thoughts, words, and actions. May I always seek to love others as he loved, and may I strive to serve and give of myself as he did.

I pray for the power of your love to transform my life, and for the grace to overcome the challenges and temptations that may come my way. May I turn to you in times of need, and may I find rest and peace in your loving arms.

I pray that my life may be a reflection of your love, and that it may bring joy and hope to all those who encounter it. May I seek to follow Christ, and may I know the fullness of your love in every moment.

In your holy name I pray, Amen.

7. A Prayer For Holy Spirit

Dear God,

I thank you for the gift of the Holy Spirit, and for the opportunity to be guided and empowered by your presence.

I pray for the manifestation of the Holy Spirit in my life, that I may be filled with your love, joy, and peace. May I be guided by your wisdom and discernment, and may I have the courage and boldness to speak and act in your name.

I pray for the power of the Holy Spirit to transform my life, and for the grace to overcome the challenges and temptations that may come my way. May I turn to you in times of need, and may I find rest and peace in your loving arms.

I pray that my life may be a reflection of the Holy Spirit, and that it may bring joy and hope to all those who encounter it. May I always seek to be guided by the Holy Spirit, and may I know the fullness of your love in every moment.

In your holy name I pray, Amen.

8. A Prayer For A Godly Character

Dear God,

I come to you today with a heart full of love and gratitude for your constant presence in my life. I thank you for your love and grace, and for the opportunity to grow in your image and likeness.

I pray for the development of a godly character in my life, that I may become more like Christ in my thoughts, words, and actions. May I be guided by your wisdom and discernment, and may I have the courage and boldness to speak and act in your name.

I pray for the power of your love to transform my life, and for the grace to overcome the challenges and temptations that may come my way. May I turn to you in times of need, and may I find rest and peace in your loving arms.

I pray that my life may be a reflection of your love and grace, and that it may bring joy and hope to all those who encounter it. May I always seek to grow in my relationship with you, and may I know the fullness of your love in every moment. In your holy name I pray, Amen.

9. A Prayer To Find Kind Words

Dear God,

I know that my words have the power to build up or tear down, and I pray for your help in choosing kind and loving words.

I pray for the wisdom to think before I speak, and for the grace to choose words that are uplifting and encouraging. May I be mindful of the impact my words have on others, and may I strive to speak words of love and compassion.

I pray for the strength and courage to overcome any negative habits or patterns in my communication, and for the grace to apologize when I have spoken in a way that is hurtful or unkind. May I seek to build others up with my words, and may I be a source of positivity and encouragement in the world.

I pray that my words may be a reflection of your love and grace, and that they may bring joy and hope to all those who encounter them. May I seek to use kind and loving words, and may I know the fullness of your love in every moment. In your holy name I pray, Amen.

10. A Prayer To Help With Anger

Dear God,

I know that anger and frustration can be destructive and harmful, and I pray for your help in managing and overcoming them.

I pray for the wisdom to understand the root causes of my anger, and for the grace to find healthy and constructive ways to deal with it. May I have the courage and strength to seek help and support when I need it, and may I find peace and healing in your love.

I pray for the power of your love to transform my heart and mind, and for the grace to overcome any negative patterns or habits that contribute to my anger. May I always strive to be patient and understanding, and may I seek to bring love and compassion to all those I encounter.

I pray that my life may be a reflection of your love and grace, and that it may bring joy and hope to all those who encounter it. May I always seek to manage my anger in a healthy and constructive way, and may I know the fullness of your love in every moment. In your holy name I pray, Amen.

11. A Prayer To Help with Jealousy

Dear God,

I am struggling with jealousy and envy. I know that these emotions can be destructive and harmful, and I pray for your help in managing and overcoming them.

I pray for the wisdom to understand the root causes of my jealousy, and for the grace to find healthy and constructive ways to deal with it. May I have the courage and strength to seek help and support when I need it, and may I find peace and healing in your love.

I pray for the power of your love to transform my heart and mind, and for the grace to overcome any negative patterns or habits that contribute to my jealousy. May I always strive to be grateful and content, and may I seek to bring love and compassion to all those I encounter.

I pray that my life may be a reflection of your love and grace, and that it may bring joy and hope to all those who encounter it. May I always seek to manage my jealousy in a healthy and constructive way, and may I know the fullness of your love in every moment.

In your holy name I pray, Amen.

12. A Prayer Of Gratitude

Dear God,

I thank you for your endless love and mercy, and for the countless blessings you have bestowed upon my life.

I am grateful for the people in my life who love and support me, and for the opportunities you have given me to grow and learn. I am thankful for the simple joys and pleasures of daily life, and for the beauty and wonder of your creation.

I am also grateful for the challenges and hardships that have come my way, for they have helped me to grow in strength and character. I know that you are with me in every moment, and I am grateful for your constant presence and guidance.

I pray that my heart may always be filled with gratitude and thankfulness, and that I may show my appreciation to others in all that I do. May I be a source of joy and hope for those around me, and may I always seek to serve and give of myself to others.

In your holy name I pray, Amen.

13. A Prayer For Difficult Times

Dear God,

know that you are with me in every moment, and I pray for your strength and guidance as I navigate these challenges.

I pray for the wisdom to understand your plan for my life, and for the grace to trust in your will even when things are difficult. May I have the courage and strength to face each day with hope and determination, and may I find comfort and peace in your loving arms.

I pray for the power of your love to transform my heart and mind, and for the grace to overcome any negative patterns or habits that may be hindering my progress. May I strive to be resilient and optimistic, and may I seek to bring love and compassion to all those I encounter.

I pray that my life may be a reflection of your love and grace, and that it may bring joy and hope to all those who encounter it. May I find strength and resilience in difficult times, and may I know the fullness of your love in every moment. In your holy name I pray, Amen.

14. A Prayer To Love

Dear God,

I come to you today with a heart full of love and gratitude for all that you have given me. I thank you for the love that surrounds me, and for the people in my life who bring joy and happiness to my days.

I pray for the power of your love to transform my life, and for the grace to share it generously with those around me. May I be a source of love and compassion for others, and bring joy and happiness to those in need.

I pray for the strength and courage to love others even in the face of difficulty, and for the wisdom to navigate the challenges of relationships. May I find hope and healing in your love, and know that you are with me every step of the way.

I pray that my love may be a reflection of your love, and that it may bring joy and hope to all those who encounter it. May I always seek to love others as you have loved me, and may I know the fullness of your love in every moment.

In your holy name I pray, Amen.

15. A Prayer For A Good Job Interview

Dear loving God,

I know that you have a plan for my life, and I pray that this interview will be an opportunity for me to use my talents and abilities to serve you and to make a positive impact in the world.

I pray that you would give me the wisdom and discernment I need to answer the questions I will be asked, and that you would help me to present myself in a way that is honest and authentic. Please give me the confidence and poise I need to make a good impression, and help me to communicate my skills and qualifications effectively.

Guide me in my career choices, and help me find a job that is fulfilling and meaningful. Please give me the opportunity to use my gifts and abilities to serve you and to make a difference in the world.

I trust in your guidance and your care, and I know that you have a plan for my life. I pray that you would use this as an opportunity for me to grow and to serve you in new and meaningful ways. I pray all of these things in Jesus' name. Amen.

16. A Prayer For My Upcoming Surgery

Dear loving God,

I know that this is a time of uncertainty and that I am entrusting my well-being to the hands of medical professionals and to you. I pray that you would bless the surgeons and medical staff who will be caring for me, and that you would give them the wisdom and skill they need to perform their work effectively. Please also protect me from any complications or unforeseen events, and give me the strength and courage I need to endure this surgery.

Be with me during this time of vulnerability, and that you would give me the peace and comfort I need to face this procedure with confidence and hope. Please be with my loved ones as well, and give them the strength and courage they need to support me during this time.

I trust in your loving care and your promise to be with us in times of need. I pray that you would use this surgery as an opportunity to bring about healing and restoration in my life, and that you would use it to bring me closer to your perfect will. Thank you for your love and your grace. I pray all of these things in Jesus' name. Amen.

17. A Prayer To Trust In God

Dear God,

I know that you are faithful and loving, and I pray for the grace to put my trust in you in all things.

I pray for the wisdom to understand your plan for my life, and for the courage to follow it even when things are uncertain. May I have the strength to let go of my fears and doubts, and may I find peace and joy in your loving arms.

I pray for the power of your love to transform my heart and mind, and for the grace to overcome any negative patterns or habits that may hinder my trust in you. May I always strive to be reliant on your strength and guidance, and may I seek to bring love and compassion to all those I encounter.

I pray that my life may be a reflection of your love and grace, and that it may bring joy and hope to all those who encounter it. May I always seek to grow in trust and reliance on you, and may I know the fullness of your love in every moment.

In your holy name I pray, Amen.

18. A Prayer For My Good Health

Dear God,

I know that you are the source of all life and healing, and I pray for your help in caring for my body and mind.

I pray for the wisdom to make healthy choices in my daily life, and for the grace to follow through on them. May I have the strength and courage to take care of myself in body, mind, and spirit, and may I find peace and joy in your loving arms.

I pray for the power of your love to transform my health and well-being, and for the grace to overcome any challenges or difficulties that may come my way. May I always strive to be strong and resilient, and may I seek to bring love and compassion to all those I encounter.

I pray that my life may be a reflection of your love and grace, and that it may bring joy and hope to all those who encounter it. May I always seek to be healthy and well, and may I know the fullness of your love in every moment.

In your holy name I pray, Amen.

19. A Prayer To Feel God's Presence

Dear God,

I know that you are with me always, and I pray for the grace to be more aware of your presence in all that I do.

I pray for the wisdom to understand your plan for my life, and for the courage to follow it faithfully. May I have the strength to turn to you in times of need, and may I find peace and joy in your loving arms.

I pray for the power of your love to transform my heart and mind, and for the grace to overcome any distractions or obstacles that may hinder my awareness of your presence. May I always strive to be attuned to your leading and guidance, and may I seek to bring love and compassion to all those I encounter.

I pray that my life may be a reflection of your love and grace, and that it may bring joy and hope to all those who encounter it. May I always seek to feel your presence more fully, and may I know the fullness of your love in every moment.

In your holy name I pray, Amen.

20. A Prayer For My Broken Heart

Dear God,

I know that you are a God of healing and comfort, and I pray for your help in mending my broken heart.

I pray for the wisdom to understand the root causes of my pain, and for the grace to find healthy and constructive ways to cope with it. May I have the courage and strength to seek help and support when I need it, and may I find peace and healing in your loving arms.

I pray for the power of your love to transform my heart and mind, and for the grace to overcome any negative patterns or habits that may be hindering my healing. May I always strive to be resilient and hopeful, and may I seek to bring love and compassion to all those I encounter.

I pray that my life may be a reflection of your love and grace, and that it may bring joy and hope to all those who encounter it. May I always seek to find healing and hope in times of pain, and may I know the fullness of your love in every moment. In your holy name I pray, Amen.

21. A Prayer For Perseverance

Dear God,

I know that you are a God of strength and power, and I pray for your help in staying the course and seeing things through to the end.

I pray for the wisdom to understand your plan for my life, and for the grace to follow it faithfully. May I have the courage and strength to face challenges and setbacks with resilience and hope, and may I find peace and joy in your loving arms.

I pray for the power of your love to transform my heart and mind, and for the grace to overcome any negative patterns or habits that may hinder my perseverance. May I always strive to be tenacious and determined, and may I seek to bring love and compassion to all those I encounter.

I pray that my life may be a reflection of your love and grace, and that it may bring joy and hope to all those who encounter it. May I always seek to persevere and stay the course, and may I know the fullness of your love in every moment. In your holy name I pray, Amen.

22. A Prayer For Self Control

Dear God,

I pray for your help in managing my thoughts, words, and actions.

I pray for the wisdom to understand the importance of self-control, and for the grace to practice it in my daily life. May I have the courage and strength to resist temptation and make healthy choices, and may I find peace and joy in your loving arms.

I pray for the power of your love to transform my heart and mind, and for the grace to overcome any negative patterns or habits that may hinder my self-control. May I always strive to be disciplined and self-controlled, and may I seek to bring love and compassion to all those I encounter.

I pray that my life may be a reflection of your love and grace, and that it may bring joy and hope to all those who encounter it. May I always seek to practice self-control and discipline, and may I know the fullness of your love in every moment.

In your holy name I pray, Amen.

23. A Prayer For Feelings of Unworth

Dear God,

I come to you today with a heart that is feeling unworthy and unlovable. I know that you are a God of love and grace, and I pray for your help in overcoming these negative feelings.

I pray for the wisdom to understand my worth and value as one of your beloved children, and for the grace to believe it in my heart. May I have the courage and strength to seek healing and forgiveness for any past mistakes or regrets, and may I find peace and joy in your loving arms.

I pray for the power of your love to transform my heart and mind, and for the grace to overcome any negative patterns or habits that may hinder my sense of self-worth.

I pray that my life may be a reflection of your love and grace, and that it may bring joy and hope to all those who encounter it. May I always seek to know and believe my worth and value in your eyes, and may I know the fullness of your love in every moment. In your holy name I pray, Amen.

24. A Prayer For Healthy Eating

Dear God,

I know that you are the source of all life and nourishment, and I pray for your help in making healthy choices.

I pray for the wisdom to understand the importance of good nutrition, and for the grace to follow through on healthy eating habits. May I have the courage and strength to resist temptation and make healthy choices, and may I find peace and joy in your loving arms.

I pray for the power of your love to transform my habits and choices, and for the grace to overcome any negative patterns or habits that may hinder my health. May I always strive to be mindful of my nutrition and make healthy choices, and may I seek to bring love and compassion to all those I encounter.

I pray that my life may be a reflection of your love and grace, and that it may bring joy and hope to all those who encounter it. May I always seek to nourish my body with healthy and nutritious foods, and may I know the fullness of your love in every moment. In your holy name I pray, Amen.

25. A Prayer For Self Doubt

Dear God,

I come to you today with a heart that is struggling with self-doubt and insecurity. I know that you are a God of love and grace, and I pray for your help in overcoming these negative feelings.

I pray for the wisdom to understand my worth and value as one of your beloved children, and for the grace to believe it in my heart. May I have the courage and strength to seek healing and forgiveness for any past mistakes or regrets, and may I find peace and joy in your loving arms.

I pray for the power of your love to transform my heart and mind, and for the grace to overcome any negative patterns or habits that may hinder my confidence and self-worth. May I always strive to be secure in your love and acceptance, and may I seek to bring love and compassion to all those I encounter.

I pray that my life may be a reflection of your love and grace, and that it may bring joy and hope to all those who encounter it. In your holy name I pray, Amen.

Prayers For My Friends and Family

26. A Prayer To Show Love

Dear God,

I pray for the wisdom to understand the needs and desires of my loved ones, and for the grace to be patient, understanding, and loving towards them. May I have the courage and strength to set boundaries and make difficult decisions when necessary, and may I always seek to bring joy and happiness to those around me.

I pray for the power of your love to transform my relationships, and for the grace to overcome any conflicts or challenges that may arise. May I always strive to be a source of support and encouragement for my loved ones, and may I seek to bring love and compassion to all those I encounter.

I pray that my relationships may be a reflection of your love and grace, and that they may bring joy and hope to all those who encounter them. May I always seek to be a good parent, sibling, and child, and may I know the fullness of your love in every moment.

In your holy name I pray, Amen.

27. A Prayer For Concerns About Safety

Dear loving God,

I come before you today with a heart full of concern for the safety and security of myself and those I love. I know that this world can be a dangerous place, and that there are many threats and dangers that we face on a daily basis.

I pray that you would protect them from harm, and that you would keep us safe from all dangers. Please give us the wisdom and discernment we need to make good decisions and to avoid risky situations.

Provide for our physical and emotional needs and give us the resources and support we need to live safe and secure lives. Please be with us in times of crisis and uncertainty, and give us the strength and courage we need to face whatever challenges may come our way.

Most of all, I pray that you would give us a sense of peace and security, knowing that you are with us always and that you have a plan for our lives. Thank you for your loving care and your constant protection. I trust in your goodness and your faithfulness, and I pray all of these things in Jesus' name. Amen.

28. A Prayer For Upcoming Surgery

Dear loving God,

I come before you today with a heart full of concern for a loved one who is preparing for surgery. I know that this is a time of uncertainty and that they are entrusting their well-being to the hands of medical professionals and to you.

Bless the surgeons and medical staff who will be caring for them giving them the wisdom and skill they need to perform their work effectively. Please protect my loved one from complications or unforeseen events, and give them the strength they need to endure this surgery.

I ask that you would be with them during this time of vulnerability. Please be with their loved ones as well, and give us all the strength and courage we need to support them during this time.

I trust in your loving care and your promise to be with us in times of need. I pray that you would use this surgery as an opportunity to bring about healing and restoration in their life, and that you would use it to bring them closer to your perfect will. I pray these things in Jesus' name. Amen.

29. A Prayer For My Pet's Health

Dear God,

I come to you today with a heart full of gratitude for the joy and companionship that my pets bring to my life. I thank you for the health and well-being of my pets, and for the blessings they bring to me every day.

I pray for their continued good health, that they may live long and happy lives by your side. May they be protected from harm and illness, and may they always be a source of love and joy for me and my family.

I pray that you will bless my pets with your presence and your love, and that you will watch over them and keep them safe. May they always know your love and care, and may they be a blessing to those around them.

In your holy name I pray, Amen.

30. A Prayer For My Pet's Happiness

Dear God,

I come to you today with a heart full of gratitude for the joy and companionship that my pets bring to my life. I thank you for the love and happiness that my pets bring me every day, and for the blessings they are in my life.

I pray for their continued happiness and well-being, that they may always find joy and contentment in their daily lives. May they be protected from harm and illness, and may they always have the love and care they need to thrive.

I pray that you will bless my pets with your presence and your love, and that you will watch over them and keep them safe. May they always know your love and care, and may they be a blessing to those around them.

I also pray for the strength and courage to be the best pet owner I can be, that I may always be there for my pets and provide them with the love and care they deserve. May we always have a strong and loving bond, and may our love for each other continue to grow.

In your holy name I pray, Amen.

31. A Prayer For Those Who Left Us

Dear loving God,

I often think of those who are no longer with us in this world. I miss them deeply and long for the opportunity to be reunited with them someday.

I know that you are the God of all comfort, and that you are close to those who are grieving. I pray that you would bring peace and comfort to those struggling with loss. Give them the strength and courage they need to face each day, and the hope and assurance they need to know that you are with them always.

I pray that you would welcome those who have passed on into your loving arms. I know that you have prepared a place for them in your kingdom, and that you are welcoming them home with open arms. Please give them rest and peace, and let them know that they are not forgotten.

I trust in your loving care and your promise of eternal life, and I know that one day I will be reunited with my loved ones in your presence. Thank you for your love and your grace. Amen.

32. A Prayer For Recovery

Dear God,

I come to you today with a heavy heart, lifting up a friend or family member who is struggling with substance abuse. I know that this is a difficult and painful journey, and I pray for your healing and restoration for them.

I pray for the strength and courage to seek help and support, and for the wisdom to make positive choices that will lead to healing and recovery. May they find hope and healing in your love, and may they know that they are not alone in this struggle.

I pray for the people in their life who love and care for them, that we may be a source of support and encouragement as they navigate this difficult journey. May we be patient, kind, and understanding as we offer our love and support.

I pray for the power of your love to transform their life, and for the grace to overcome the challenges they are facing. May they find strength and hope in you, and may they know that you are with them every step of the way. In your holy name I pray, Amen.

33. A Prayer For Those Struggling With Loss

Dear God,

I come to you today to pray for someone struggling with loss. I know that this is a difficult and painful time, and I pray for your comfort and peace for them.

I pray for the strength and courage to face each day, and for the wisdom to navigate their grief and find healing in your love. May they find hope and comfort in the knowledge that you are with them, and that you understand their pain and sorrow.

I pray for the people in their life who love and care for them, that we may be a source of support and encouragement as they navigate this difficult time. May we be patient, kind, and understanding as we offer our love and support.

I pray for the power of your love to bring healing and restoration to their broken heart, and for the grace to overcome the challenges they are facing. May they find strength and hope in you, and may they know that you are with them every step of the way.

In your holy name I pray, Amen.

34. A Prayer For Healing

Dear God,

I come to you today with a heart full of hope and a desire for healing for (name). I lift them up to you, asking for your mercy and grace to be upon them.

I pray for physical healing for (name), that you would restore their body to health and strength. I pray for emotional and mental healing as well, that you would bring peace and comfort to their mind and heart.

I pray for your presence and your love to surround (name), that they may feel your comfort and peace in the midst of their struggle. May they know that they are not alone, and that you are with them every step of the way.

I pray for the strength and courage to face each day, and for the wisdom to navigate their journey towards healing. May they find hope and healing in your love, and may they know that you are always with them.

In your holy name I pray, Amen.

35. A Prayer For Success

Dear God,

I come to you today with a heart full of hope and a desire for success for (name). I lift them up to you, asking for your guidance and support as they pursue their goals and dreams.

I pray that they make wise and thoughtful decisions on their path towards success. May they have the strength and courage to overcome any challenges that may come their way, and may they persevere through difficulties with grace and determination.

I pray for your presence and your love to surround (name), that they may feel your support and encouragement as they work towards their goals. May they know that they are not alone, and that you are with them every step of the way.

I pray for your blessings to be upon (name), that they may find success and fulfillment in all that they do. May they be a source of inspiration and joy for those around them, and may they know that their hard work and dedication is greatly appreciated. In your holy name I pray, Amen.

36. A Prayer For Divine Guidance

Dear God,

I thank you for the love and support they bring me every day, and for the blessings they are in my life.

I pray for your guidance and wisdom for my friends and family, that they may make wise and thoughtful decisions on their path through life. May they have the strength and courage to overcome any challenges that may come their way, and may they persevere through difficulties with grace and determination.

I pray for your presence and your love to surround them, that they may feel your support and encouragement as they navigate the ups and downs of life. May they know that they are not alone, and that you are with them every step of the way.

I pray for your blessings to be upon them, that they may find success and fulfillment in all that they do. May they be a source of inspiration and joy for those around them, and may they know that their hard work and dedication is greatly appreciated.

In your holy name I pray, Amen.

37. A Prayer Of Blessings

Dear God,

I come to you with gratitude for the friends and family in my life. I thank you for the love and support they bring me every day, and for the blessings they are in my life.

I pray for your blessings to be upon my friends and family, that they may experience your love and grace in all that they do. May they find success and fulfillment in their endeavors, and may they know your peace and joy in every moment.

I pray for your protection and guidance for my friends and family, that they may be kept safe from harm and may always find direction and purpose in life. May they be a source of love and support for those around them, and may they always be a blessing to those in need.

I pray that my friends and family may always feel your presence and your love, and that they may know that you are with them every step of the way. May they be a light to those around them, and may they bring joy and happiness wherever they go. In your holy name I pray, Amen.

38. A Prayer For A Friend Losing Faith

Dear God,

I come to you today with a heavy heart, lifting up a friend who is struggling with their faith. I know that this is a difficult and painful time for them, and I pray for your comfort and peace for them.

I pray for the strength and courage to face each day, and for the wisdom to navigate their doubts and questions. May they find hope and healing in your love, and may they know that they are not alone in this struggle.

I pray for the people in their life who love and care for them, that we may be a source of support and encouragement as they navigate this difficult time. May we be patient, kind, and understanding as we offer our love and support.

I pray for the power of your love to bring healing and restoration to their broken heart, and for the grace to overcome the challenges they are facing. May they find strength and hope in you, and may they know that you are with them every step of the way.

In your holy name I pray, Amen.

39. A Prayer To Love When It's Hard

Dear God,

I know that you are a God of love and grace, and I pray for your help in cultivating love and forgiveness towards my loved ones. May I have the courage and strength to let go of resentment and anger, and may I find peace and joy in your loving arms.

I pray for the power of your love to transform my heart and mind, and for the grace to overcome any negative patterns or habits that may hinder my ability to love and forgive. May I always strive to be loving and kind towards my family, and may I seek to bring love and compassion to all those I encounter.

I pray that my life may be a reflection of your love and grace, and that it may bring joy and hope to all those who encounter it. May I always seek to cultivate love and forgiveness towards my family, and may I know the fullness of your love in every moment.

In your holy name I pray, Amen.

40. A Prayer For A Peaceful Home

Dear God,

I know that you are a God of love and grace, and I pray for your help in creating a peaceful and loving atmosphere in my home.

I pray for the wisdom to understand the importance of peace and harmony in the home, and for the grace to practice it in my daily life. May I have the courage and strength to let go of resentment and anger, and may I find peace and joy in your loving arms.

I pray for the power of your love to transform the hearts and minds of all those in my home, and for the grace to overcome any conflicts or misunderstandings that may arise. May we all strive to be loving and kind towards one another, and may we seek to bring love and compassion to all those we encounter.

I pray that my home may be a reflection of your love and grace, and that it may bring joy and hope to all those who enter it. May we all seek to cultivate peace and harmony in our home, and may we know the fullness of your love in every moment. In your holy name I pray, Amen.

41. A Prayer For Restoring Relationships

I come to you today with a heart that is seeking restoration in my relationships. I know that you are a God of love and grace, and I pray for your help in healing and reconciling with those I have been at odds with.

May I have the courage and strength to let go of resentment and anger, and may I find peace and joy in your loving arms.

I pray for the power of your love to transform the hearts and minds of all those involved in these relationships, and for the grace to overcome any conflicts or misunderstandings that may be hindering restoration. May we all strive to be loving and forgiving towards one another, and may we seek to bring love and compassion to all those we encounter.

I pray that my relationships may be a reflection of your love and grace, and that they may bring joy and hope to all those involved. May we all seek to restore and reconcile with one another, and may we know the fullness of your love in every moment.

In your holy name I pray, Amen.

42. A Prayer For Meals

Dear God,

As we gather together to enjoy this meal, we come to you with hearts full of gratitude and thankfulness. We are blessed to have food to nourish our bodies and the opportunity to share this time together.

We thank you for your provision and for the abundance of blessings that you have given us. We are grateful for your love and grace, and for the many ways you have shown it to us.

We pray that this meal would be a time of joy and fellowship, and that it would bring us closer together as a family. May we always remember to be thankful for the many blessings you have given us, and may we seek to share your love and grace with all those we encounter.

We pray this in your holy name, Amen.

43. A Prayer For Bedtime

Dear God,

As I lay down to rest, I come to you with a heart full of gratitude and trust. I thank you for the many blessings of this day and for your constant presence in my life.

I pray for your peace and protection to surround me as I sleep, and for your wisdom and guidance to guide me in my dreams. May I rest in your loving arms and wake up feeling refreshed and renewed.

I pray for those who are in need of your love and care, and for your healing and restoration in their lives. May your love and grace be present in all the world, and may we all know your peace and joy.

I trust in your goodness and faithfulness, and I give you my day and my night. In your holy name I pray, Amen.

44. A Prayer For Our Visitors

Dear God,

As we welcome our visitors into our home and community, we come to you with hearts full of gratitude and hospitality. We thank you for the opportunity to share your love and grace with those who have joined us, and we pray for your guidance and wisdom as we seek to serve them.

We pray for your protection and provision for our visitors, and for your healing and restoration in their lives. May they experience your love and kindness in all that we do, and may they feel welcomed and valued as part of our community.

We pray for your guidance and direction as we seek to be good stewards of your gifts and resources, and for your wisdom and discernment as we make decisions that impact our visitors. May we always seek to serve and honor you, and may we bring joy and hope to all those we encounter.

We pray this in your holy name, Amen.

45. A Prayer Before Travel

Dear God,

As we prepare to embark on this journey, we come to you with hearts full of excitement and anticipation. We thank you for the opportunity to see new places and experience new cultures, and we pray for your protection and provision as we travel.

We pray for your guidance and wisdom as we navigate unfamiliar environments and situations, and for your grace and patience as we encounter challenges and difficulties. May we always seek to honor you and serve others, and may we bring joy and hope to all those we encounter.

We pray for your protection and care for our families and loved ones while we are away, and for your provision and grace in all their needs. May we always remember to stay connected and communicate with them, and may we return home with grateful hearts.

We trust in your goodness and faithfulness, and we give you this journey and all that it entails. In your holy name we pray, Amen.

46. A Prayer For Reconciliation

Dear God,

We come to you today seeking reconciliation and healing. You are a God of love and grace, and we pray for your help in mending broken relationships.

May we have the courage and strength to let go of resentment and anger. We pray for the power of your love to transform the hearts and minds of all those involved and for the grace to overcome any conflicts or misunderstandings that may be hindering reconciliation. May we all strive to be loving and forgiving towards one another, and may we seek to bring love and compassion to all those we encounter.

We pray that our relationships may be a reflection of your love and grace, and that they may bring joy and hope to all those involved. May we all seek to reconcile and restore peace and harmony, and may we know the fullness of your love in every moment.

In your holy name we pray, Amen.

47. A Prayer For A Loving Family

Dear God,

We know that you are a God of love and grace, and we pray for your help in creating a home that is full of love and joy.

We pray for the wisdom to understand the importance of loving and respecting one another, and for the grace to practice it in our daily lives. May we have the courage and strength to let go of resentment and anger, and may we find peace and joy in your loving arms.

We pray for the power of your love to transform our hearts and minds, and for the grace to overcome any conflicts or misunderstandings that may arise. May we all strive to be loving and kind towards one another, and may we seek to bring love and compassion to all those we encounter.

We pray that our home may be a reflection of your love and grace, and that it may bring joy and hope to all those who are a part of it. May we always seek to cultivate love and unity in our family, and may we know the fullness of your love in every moment. In your holy name we pray, Amen.

48. A Prayer For A New Family Member

Dear God,

We come to you today with hearts that are full of joy and excitement as we welcome a new member into our family. We thank you for the gift of this new life, and for the opportunity to love and nurture them.

We pray for your protection and provision for our new family member, and for your guidance and wisdom as we care for them. May we always strive to be loving and compassionate towards them, and may we seek to bring them up in your love and grace.

We pray for your guidance and direction as we navigate this new role as a family, and for your wisdom and discernment as we make decisions that impact our new family member. May we always seek to honor you and serve others, and may we bring joy and hope to all those we encounter.

We trust in your goodness and faithfulness, and we give you this new family member and all that they bring. In your holy name we pray, Amen.

49. A Prayer To Find Gratitude

Dear God,

We pray for your wisdom and guidance as I seek to cultivate gratitude in our hearts. May we open our eyes to the good things in our lives, and find joy and contentment in all that you have given us.

We pray for the strength and courage to overcome the struggles and challenges that are weighing us down, and for the grace to find hope and joy in the midst of difficult times. May we always turn to you in times of need, and may we find rest and peace in your loving arms.

We pray that our hearts may be filled with gratitude and thankfulness, and that we may show my appreciation to others in all that we do. May we be a source of joy and hope for those around us, and may we always seek to serve and give of ourselves to others. In your holy name we pray, Amen.

50. A Prayer To Make Nice

Dear God,

We pray for the wisdom to understand the importance of showing love and compassion towards others, and for the grace to practice it in our daily lives. May we have the courage and strength to let go of negativity and judgment, and may we find peace and joy in your loving arms.

We pray for the power of your love to transform our hearts and minds, and for the grace to overcome any habits or patterns that may hinder our ability to be kind and compassionate. May we always strive to be loving and kind towards others, and may we seek to bring love and compassion to all those we encounter.

We pray that our lives may be a reflection of your love and grace, and that we may bring joy and hope to all those we encounter. May we always seek to cultivate kindness and compassion, and may we know the fullness of your love in every moment.

In your holy name we pray, Amen.

Prayers For My Community

51. A Prayer For Our Community Leaders

Dear loving God,

I know the leaders of our community have a difficult and important job, and that they are responsible for making decisions that impact the lives of so many people.

I pray that you would guide them with wisdom and integrity, and that you would give them the insight and discernment they need to make good decisions. Please help them to put the needs of the community before their own interests, and to work for the common good.

I also pray that you would give them the strength and courage they need to face the challenges and difficulties that come with leadership. Please be with them as they navigate the complexities of their roles, and give them the support and encouragement they need to serve effectively.

I know that you have called them to lead, and I pray that you would use them to make a positive impact on our community. Thank you for your love and your grace. I pray all of these things in Jesus' name. Amen.

52. A Prayer For A Safe Community

Dear loving God,

I know that there are many threats and dangers that we face on a daily basis, and I pray that you would protect us from harm.

Please bless the police and other emergency responders who work to keep our community safe, and give them the wisdom and discernment they need to do their jobs effectively. I also pray that you would give us the wisdom and discernment we need to make good decisions and to avoid risky situations.

I ask that you would be with us in times of crisis and uncertainty, and that you would give us the strength and courage we need to face whatever challenges may come our way. Please also bring healing and restoration to those who have been harmed or traumatized by violence or other dangers.

Most of all, I pray that you would give us a sense of peace and security, knowing that you are with us always and that you have a plan for our lives. Thank you for your loving care and your constant protection. I pray all of these things in Jesus' name. Amen.

53. A Prayer For Our Schools

Dear loving God,

I know that our schools are important for the development of our young people, and I pray that they would be places of learning, safety, and growth.

I pray that you would bless the teachers and administrators who work in these institutions, and that you would give them the wisdom and inspiration they need to educate and inspire their students. Please also bless the students with a love of learning, and help them to find joy and purpose in their studies.

I also pray that you would provide the resources and support that these schools need to be effective and successful. Please be with those who are working to improve the education system, and give them the vision and guidance they need to make a positive impact.

I know that you are the source of all knowledge and wisdom, and I pray that you would use these schools as places of growth and transformation for the students and communities they serve. Thank you for your love and your grace. I pray all of these things in Jesus' name. Amen.

54. A Prayer For Our Local Businesses

Dear loving God,

I pray that you would bless the owners and employees of the businesses and organizations in ur community, and that you would give them the wisdom and discernment they need to be successful. Please also bless the customers and clients of these entities, and help them to find value and satisfaction in their interactions.

I also pray that you would provide the resources and support that these businesses and organizations need to grow and thrive. Please be with those who are working to improve the local economy, and give them the vision and guidance they need to make a positive impact.

I know that you are the source of all abundance and prosperity, and I pray that you would use these businesses and organizations as a means of blessing and enriching our community. Thank you for your love and your grace. I pray all of these things in Jesus' name. Amen.

55. A Prayer For Our Healthcare Community

Dear loving God,

I come before you today to pray for our doctors and nurses. I know that they are responsible for the well-being and health of so many people, and I pray that they would be able to provide excellent care to those in need.

I pray that you would bless the doctors, nurses, and other healthcare professionals who work in these facilities, and that you would give them the wisdom and skill they need to heal and restore those who are suffering. Please also bless the patients and their families, and give them the strength and courage they need to face their challenges. I also pray that you would provide the resources and support that these healthcare professionals and facilities need to be effective and successful.

I know that you are the source of all healing and health, and I pray that you would use these healthcare professionals and facilities as a means of bringing about restoration and well-being for those who are in need. Thank you for your love and your grace. I pray all of these things in Jesus' name. Amen.

56. A Prayer For Our Local Churches

Dear loving God,

I pray that you would bless the pastors and other leaders of these communities, and that you would give them the wisdom and discernment they need to guide and inspire their congregations. Please also bless the members of these communities, and help them to grow in their faith and to find support and encouragement in their journey.

I also pray that you would provide the resources and support that these churches and faith communities need to be effective and successful. Please be with those who are working to spread the Gospel and to build up the body of Christ, and give them the vision and guidance they need to make a positive impact.

I know that you are the source of all truth and wisdom, and I pray that you would use these churches and faith communities as a means of bringing about spiritual growth and transformation for those who are seeking you. Thank you for your love and your grace. I pray all of these things in Jesus' name. Amen.

57. A Prayer For Our Community's Families

Dear God,

I pray that you would bless the parents and children in our community, and that you would give them the wisdom and discernment they need to navigate the challenges and joys of family life. Please also help them to find support and encouragement in their relationships with one another, and to build strong bonds of love and commitment.

I also pray that you would provide the resources and support that these families need to be effective and successful. Please be with those who are working to strengthen and support families, and give them the vision and guidance they need to make a positive impact.

I know that you are a God of love and grace, and I pray that you would use these families as a means of bringing about healing and restoration for all of us. Thank you for your love and your grace. I pray all of these things in Jesus' name. Amen.

58. A Prayer For Our Seniors

Dear loving God,

I pray that you would bless the seniors in our community with good health and vitality. Give them the strength and energy they need to enjoy their golden years and help them to find companionship and connection.

I also pray that you would provide the resources and support that these seniors need to be able to live independently and with dignity. Please be with those who are working to improve the quality of life for seniors, and give them the vision and guidance they need to make a positive impact.

I know that you are a God of compassion and love, and I pray that you would use these seniors as a means of bringing about joy and fulfillment for all of us. Thank you for your love and your grace. I pray all of these things in Jesus' name. Amen.

59. A Prayer For Artists And Creators

Dear loving God,

I pray that you would bless the artists and creative people in our community with your inspiration, and that you would give them the motivation and energy they need to create and share their work. Please also help them to find support and encouragement from others, and to feel valued and appreciated for their contributions.

I also pray that you would provide the resources and support that these artists and creative people need to be able to share their talents and make a positive impact. Please be with those who are working to support and promote the arts in our community, and give them the vision and guidance they need to make a positive impact.

I know that you are the source of all creativity and beauty, and I pray that you would use these artists and creative people as a means of bringing about joy and enrichment for all of us. Thank you for your love and your grace. I pray all of these things in Jesus' name. Amen.

60. A Prayer For Our First Responders

Dear loving God,

I pray that you would bless the emergency responders and public servants in our community with strength and courage, and that you would give them the wisdom and discernment they need to do their jobs effectively. Please also help them to find support and encouragement from others, and to feel valued and appreciated for their contributions.

I also pray that you would provide the resources and support that these emergency responders and public servants need to be able to serve with excellence and dedication. Please be with those who are working to support and improve the emergency response and public service systems, and give them the vision and guidance they need to make a positive impact.

I know that you are a God of justice and compassion, and I pray that you would use these emergency responders and public servants as a means of bringing about safety and security for all of us. Thank you for your love and your grace. I pray all of these things in Jesus' name. Amen.

61. A Prayer For Journalists

Dear loving God,

I pray that you would bless the journalists and media in our community with wisdom and discernment, and that you would give them the courage and conviction they need to report the truth. I know that these are people who are responsible for informing the public and holding those in power accountable, and I pray that they would be able to do so with integrity and accuracy. Please also help them to find support and encouragement from others, and to feel valued and appreciated for their contributions.

I also pray that you would provide the resources and support that these journalists and media need to be able to report the truth and inform the public.

I know that you are a God of truth and justice, and I pray that you would use these journalists and media as a means of bringing about transparency and accountability in our society. Thank you for your love and your grace. I pray all of these things in Jesus' name. Amen.

62. A Prayer For Politicians

Dear loving God,

I pray that you would bless the political leaders in our community with wisdom and discernment, and that you would give them the insight and vision they need to make good decisions. Please also help them to put the needs of the community before their own interests, and to work for the common good.

I also pray that you would provide the resources and support that these political leaders need to be able to lead effectively. Please be with those who are working to improve the political process and to hold our leaders accountable, and give them the vision and guidance they need to make a positive impact.

I know that you are a God of justice and righteousness, and I pray that you would use these political leaders as a means of bringing about positive change and progress in our community. Thank you for your love and your grace. I pray all of these things in Jesus' name. Amen.

63. A Prayer For Local Farmers

Dear loving God,

I pray that you would bless the farmers in our area with good weather and healthy crops, and that you would give them the wisdom and discernment they need to manage their land and their animals. Please also help them to find support and encouragement from others, and to feel valued and appreciated for their contributions.

I know that these are people who work hard every day to provide food and resources for our community, and I pray that they would be able to do so with success and prosperity. I pray that you would provide the resources and support that these farmers need to be able to farm successfully.

I know that you are the source of all abundance and prosperity, and I pray that you would use these farmers as a means of bringing about health and nourishment for our community. Thank you for your love and your grace. I pray all of these things in Jesus' name. Amen.

64. A Prayer For Mental Well Being

Dear loving God,

I pray that you would bring healing and hope to those who are suffering. I pray that you would bless the people in our community with peace and joy, and that you would give them the strength and resilience they need to cope with life's challenges. Please also help them to find support and encouragement from others, and to feel valued and appreciated for who they are.

I also pray that you would provide the resources and support that people in our community need to be able to address their mental health needs. Please be with those who are working to improve mental health services and to promote awareness and understanding of mental health issues, and give them the vision and guidance they need to make a positive impact.

I know that you are a God of love and compassion, and I pray that you would use your healing power to bring about hope and restoration for those who are struggling emotionally and mentally. Thank you for your love and your grace. I pray all of these things in Jesus' name. Amen.

65. A Prayer For Spiritual Growth In The Community

Dear God,

I come to you today with a heart full of gratitude and a desire for spiritual growth. I thank you for the blessings you have given me, and for the people in my community who support and encourage me on my spiritual journey.

I pray for the strength and courage to seek out opportunities for deeper connection with you. Help me to be open to your guidance and to the promptings of the Holy Spirit.

I pray for the growth and well-being of my community, that we may all come closer to you and to one another. May we be a source of love, support, and encouragement for one another as we seek to grow in our faith.

I pray that you will bless our community with your presence and your love, and that we may be a light to those around us.

In your holy name I pray, Amen.

66. A Prayer For Happiness, Love, And Joy In The Community

Dear God,

I thank you for the blessings you have given us, and for the people in my community who bring light and happiness into my life.

I pray for the happiness and well-being of my community, that we may all find joy and contentment in our daily lives. May we be a source of love, support, and encouragement for one another as we seek to find happiness and fulfillment.

I pray that you will bless our community with your presence and your love, and that we may be a light to those around us. May we be a beacon of hope and joy in times of hardship, and may we always remember to give thanks for the blessings you have given us.

In your holy name I pray, Amen.

67. A Prayer For Community Connection

Dear God,

I thank you for the people in my life who support and encourage me, and for the sense of belonging that I feel as a part of this community.

I pray for the connections and relationships within our community, that we may all find a sense of belonging and support. May we be a source of love, kindness, and compassion for one another, and may we always strive to build each other up.

I pray that you will bless our community with your presence and your love, and that we may be a light to those around us. May we be a beacon of hope and support for those who are seeking connection and community.

In your holy name I pray, Amen.

68. A Prayer During Disaster

Dear God,

We know that you are a God of love and grace, and we pray for your help in navigating this difficult and uncertain time.

We pray for your protection and provision for those who have been affected by the disaster, and for your healing and restoration in their lives. May they find comfort and hope in your loving arms, and may they know that they are not alone.

We pray for your guidance and wisdom for those who are leading and coordinating the response and recovery efforts, and for your grace and strength for all those who are working to bring aid and assistance to those in need.

We pray that our community may be a reflection of your love and grace, and that we may find strength and unity as we come together to support one another. May we always remember to turn to you in times of need, and may we know the fullness of your love in every moment.

In your holy name we pray, Amen.

69. A Prayer For Our Young Adults

Dear God,

We know that you are a God of love and grace, and we pray for your help in guiding and nurturing the young adults in our community as they navigate the challenges and opportunities of this stage of life.

We pray for your wisdom and discernment as they make important decisions about their education, career, and relationships. May they seek your guidance and direction in all things, and may they find joy and purpose in your plans for their lives.

We pray for your protection and provision for these young people, and for your healing and restoration in their lives. May they find hope and strength in your loving arms, and may they know that they are not alone.

We pray that our community may be a place of support and encouragement for these young adults, and that we may all seek to be loving and compassionate towards one another. May we strive to be a positive influence in the lives of these young people, and may we bring hope and joy to all those we encounter. In your holy name we pray, Amen.

70. A Prayer For the Parents

Dear God,

We know that you are a God of love and grace, and we pray for your help in guiding and supporting the parents in our community as they raise and nurture their children.

We pray for your wisdom and discernment for these parents as they make important decisions about their children's education, health, and well-being. May they seek your guidance and direction in all things, and may they find joy and fulfillment in their roles as parents.

We pray for your protection and provision for these parents and their families, and for your healing and restoration in their lives. May they find hope and strength in your loving arms, and may they know that they are not alone.

We pray that our community may be a place of support and encouragement for these parents, and that we may all seek to be loving and compassionate towards one another. In your holy name we pray, Amen.

71. A Prayer For Our Team

Dear God,

We come to you today with hearts that are full of gratitude and appreciation for our team. We thank you for the talents and gifts of each member, and for the opportunity to work together towards a common goal.

We pray for your guidance and wisdom as we work together, and for your grace and patience as we navigate challenges and difficulties. May we always strive to be respectful and supportive of one another, and may we seek to bring excellence and integrity to all that we do.

We pray for your protection and provision for our team, and for your healing and restoration in our lives. May we find hope and strength in your loving arms, and may we know that we are not alone.

We pray that our team may be a reflection of your love and grace, and that we may bring joy and hope to all those we encounter. May we always seek to work together in unity and harmony, and may we know the fullness of your love in every moment.

In your holy name we pray, Amen.

72. A Prayer For New Years

Dear God,

We thank you for the many blessings of the past year, and we pray for your guidance and wisdom as we look towards the future.

We pray for your protection and provision for our community, and for your healing and restoration in the lives of those who are in need. May we all strive to be loving and compassionate towards one another, and may we seek to bring hope and joy to all those we encounter.

We pray for your guidance and direction as we set goals and make plans for the new year, and for your wisdom and discernment as we navigate the challenges and opportunities that come our way. May we always seek to honor you and serve others, and may we find purpose and fulfillment in all that we do.

We pray that our community may be a reflection of your love and grace, and that we may find unity and strength as we come together to support one another. May we always remember to turn to you in times of need, and may we know the fullness of your love in every moment. In your holy name we pray, Amen.

73. A Christmas Community Prayer

Dear God,

As we celebrate the birth of your son, Jesus, we thank you for the gift of salvation that he brings, and for the love and grace that he exemplifies.

We pray for your protection and provision for our community, and for your healing and restoration in the lives of those who are in need. May we all strive to be loving and compassionate towards one another, and may we seek to bring hope and joy to all those we encounter.

We pray for your guidance and direction as we celebrate the Christmas season, and for your wisdom and discernment as we navigate the challenges and opportunities that come our way. May we always seek to honor you and serve others, and may we find purpose and fulfillment in all that we do.

We pray that our community may be a reflection of your love and grace, and that we may find unity and strength as we come together to support one another. May we always remember to turn to you in times of need, and may we know the fullness of your love in every moment. In your holy name we pray, Amen

74. A Prayer For Our Neighbors

Dear God,

We come to you today with hearts that are full of concern and love for our neighbors. We know that you are a God of love and grace, and we pray for your help in fostering healthy and positive relationships with those who live near us.

We pray for your wisdom and discernment as we navigate the challenges and opportunities of living in community, and for your grace and patience as we seek to understand and respect one another. May we always strive to be loving and compassionate towards our neighbors, and may we seek to bring hope and joy to all those we encounter.

We pray for your protection and provision for our neighbors and their families, and for your healing and restoration in their lives. May they find strength in your loving arms and know they are not alone.

We pray that our community may be a reflection of your love and grace, and that we may find unity and strength as we come together to support one another. In your holy name we pray, Amen.\

75. A Prayer For The Lonely

Dear God,

We know that you are a God of love and grace, and we pray for your help in bringing comfort and hope to those who are struggling with feelings of isolation.

We pray for your healing and restoration in the lives of those who are lonely, and for your grace and strength to overcome the challenges that they are facing. May they find hope and strength in your loving arms, and may they know that they are not alone.

We pray for your wisdom and discernment as we seek to support and encourage those who are lonely, and for your guidance and direction as we navigate the challenges and opportunities of being in community.

We pray that our community may be a reflection of your love and grace, and that we may find unity and strength as we come together to support one another. May we always remember to turn to you in times of need, and may we know the fullness of your love in every moment. In your holy name we pray, Amen.

Prayers For All

76. A Prayer For Good Health For The Ill

Dear loving God,

I pray that you would touch the lives of those who are struggling with physical ailments, and that you would bring them relief and restoration. Bless them with the strength and courage they need to face their challenges.

Please also bless the medical professionals who are working to care for the sick. Give them wisdom and skill as they seek to diagnose and treat those who are suffering. I pray that you would provide them with the resources and support they need to do their jobs effectively, and that you would protect them from harm as they work to serve others.

I trust in your loving care and your ability to work wonders, and I know that you have a plan for the lives of those who are sick. I pray that you would use this time of illness to draw them closer to you and to bring them closer to your perfect will.

Thank you for your love and your mercy, and for the hope and healing you provide. I pray all of these things in Jesus' name. Amen.

77. A Prayer For The Hungry

Dear loving God,

I know that you are the provider of all things, and that you have a heart for those who are in need. I pray that you would provide for those who are hungry, both here in my own community and around the world. Please bless those who are struggling to put food on the table and meet the basic needs of their families.

I ask that you would open doors of opportunity for those who are in need of work, and that you would provide them with the resources they need to support themselves and their loved ones. Please also bless the organizations and individuals who are working to combat hunger and provide food and assistance to those in need.

I pray that you would use this time of need to bring people closer to you and to your perfect will. Please provide for those who are hungry, and use this situation to demonstrate your love for all who are in need.

Thank you for your loving care and your provision. I trust in your ability to meet the needs of all your children, and I pray all these things in Jesus' name. Amen.

78. A Prayer For World Peace

Dear loving God,

I pray that you would bring an end to all forms of violence and aggression, and that you would heal the wounds of those who have been harmed or traumatized by conflict. Please give wisdom and guidance to those who are working to bring about peace, and bless them with the resources and support they need to be successful.

I also pray that you would work in the hearts and minds of all people, helping them to overcome hatred and animosity and to cultivate love and understanding towards one another. Please help us to see each other as brothers and sisters, and to value the dignity and worth of every person.

I know that you are the prince of peace, and that you have the power to bring about transformation and reconciliation. I pray that you would use your love and your grace to bring about a world that is free from conflict and strife. Thank you for your goodness and your mercy. I pray all of these things in Jesus' name. Amen.

79. A Prayer For The Poor And Homeless

Dear loving God,

I know that there are so many people in our world who are struggling to meet their basic needs and who are without a safe and secure place to call home. I pray that you would provide for the needs of the poor and the homeless, and that you would give them the resources and support they need to lift themselves out of poverty.

I also pray that you would work in the hearts and minds of those who are struggling with poverty and homelessness, helping them to find hope and purpose. Please give them the courage and determination they need to overcome their challenges, and help them to see that they are loved and valued by you.

I know that you are a God of justice and compassion, and that you have a special concern for the poor. I pray that you would use your love and your grace to bring about a world where everyone has the opportunity to thrive and succeed. Thank you for your goodness and your mercy. I pray all of these things in Jesus' name. Amen.

80. A Prayer For Kindness To The Earth

Dear loving God,

I know that you have created the earth and all its creatures, and that you have entrusted us with the responsibility to care for and protect it.

I pray that we would treat the earth with kindness and respect, and that we would work to preserve its natural beauty and resources for future generations. Please give us the wisdom and discernment we need to make good choices that will benefit the earth and all its inhabitants.

I also pray that you would help us to learn from the mistakes of the past, and to work towards a more sustainable and environmentally-friendly future. Please give us the courage and determination we need to make the changes that are necessary, and help us to see that our actions have a ripple effect on the world around us.

I know that you have called us to be stewards of your creation, and I pray that we would take this responsibility seriously. Please use us as agents of change, and help us to make a positive impact on the world. Thank you for your love and your grace. I pray all of these things in Jesus' name. Amen.

81. A Prayer For Kindness and Respect

Dear God,

I know that you are a God of love and justice, and I pray for your help in creating a more loving and compassionate world. We pray for the wisdom to understand the importance of treating others with kindness and respect, and for the grace to practice it in my own life. May we have the courage and strength to stand up for justice and righteousness, and may we find peace and joy in your loving arms.

We pray for the power of your love to transform the hearts and minds of all people, and for the grace to overcome any prejudices or injustices that may divide us. May we all strive to be kind and respectful towards one another.

We pray that our world may be a reflection of your love and grace, and that it may bring joy and hope to all those who encounter it. May we all seek to create a world where all are treated with kindness and respect, and may we know the fullness of your love in every moment.

In your holy name I pray, Amen.

82. A Prayer For Education

Dear God,

We know that you are a God of love and grace, and we pray for your help in ensuring that all people have the opportunity to learn and grow.

We pray for your wisdom and discernment as we seek to provide access to education for all, and for your guidance and direction as we navigate the challenges and opportunities of creating equitable systems of learning. May we always strive to be loving and compassionate towards one another, and may we seek to bring hope and joy to all those we encounter.

We pray for your protection and provision for those who are denied access to education, and for your healing and restoration in their lives.

We pray that our community may be a reflection of your love and grace, and that we may find unity and strength as we come together to support one another. May we always remember to turn to you in times of need, and may we know the fullness of your love in every moment. In your holy name we pray, Amen.

83. A Prayer For Understanding

Dear God,

We know that you are a God of love and grace, and we pray for your help in fostering positive relationships and cooperation between nations.

We pray for your wisdom and discernment as we seek to understand and respect the cultures and beliefs of others, and for your grace and patience as we navigate the challenges and opportunities of living in a diverse and interconnected world. May we always strive to be loving and compassionate towards one another.

We pray for your protection and provision for those who are affected by conflict and tension between nations, and for your healing and restoration in their lives. May they find hope and strength in your loving arms, and may they know that they are not alone.

We pray that our community may be a reflection of your love and grace, and that we may find unity and strength as we come together to support one another. May we always remember to turn to you in times of need, and may we know the fullness of your love in every moment. In your holy name we pray, Amen.

84. A Prayer To Know God's Love

Dear God,

We are full of hope and desire for all people to know and experience your love. We know that you are a God of love and grace, and we pray for your help in bringing the message of your love to all corners of the earth.

We pray for your wisdom and discernment as we seek to share the good news of your love with others, and for your grace and strength as we navigate the challenges and opportunities of being ambassadors for your kingdom. May we always strive to be loving and compassionate towards one another, and may we seek to bring hope and joy to all those we encounter.

We pray for your protection and provision for those who are searching for meaning and purpose in life, and for your healing and restoration in their lives. May they find hope and strength in your loving arms, and may they know that they are not alone.

May we always remember to turn to you in times of need, and may we know the fullness of your love in every moment. In your holy name we pray, Amen.

85. A Pray For Inspiration

Dear God,

We come to you today seeking inspiration for all. We ask for your guidance and wisdom as we navigate through life's challenges and opportunities. Help us to find motivation and purpose in all that we do, and give us the strength and courage to pursue our dreams.

As we seek inspiration, help us to remember that it is not about achieving perfection, but rather about living our lives to the fullest and making a positive impact on the world around us. May we find inspiration in the simple things, in the beauty of nature, and in the kindness and love of others.

We pray that you would fill our hearts and minds with your Holy Spirit, and that we would be inspired by your love and grace. Help us to use our gifts and talents to serve you and others, and to be a light to those around us.

We ask these things in your holy name, Amen.

86. A Prayer For Connection

Dear God,

We come to you today seeking connection and community for all. We recognize that we are not meant to walk through life alone, but rather to support and lift each other up.

We pray that you would bring people into the lives of those who need it. To encourage and inspire them, and to walk alongside them through the ups and downs of life. Help us to build strong, meaningful relationships with others, and to be a source of support and love for those in need.

May we find community in the places where we worship, work, and play, and may we be a blessing to those around us. We pray that you would knit our hearts together in love, and that we would be a shining example of your love and grace to the world.

We ask these things in your holy name, Amen.

87. A Prayer For Winter Safety

Dear God,

As winter approaches, we come to you with a prayer for safety. We ask for your protection and guidance as we navigate the colder months ahead.

We pray that you would keep us safe as we travel on icy roads and shovel snow from our driveways and sidewalks. May your angels surround us and keep us from harm as we brave the elements.

We also pray for those who are vulnerable during the winter months, such as the elderly, the sick, and the homeless. We ask that you would provide for their needs and keep them safe from the cold.

May your love and care surround us as we face the challenges of winter, and may we trust in your goodness and faithfulness.

We ask these things in your holy name, Amen.

88. A Prayer For Those Away From Home

Dear God,

We lift up to you all those who are away from home today. Whether they are far from their families, friends, or communities, we ask that you would surround them with your love and care.

We pray that you would give them the strength and courage they need to face the challenges of being away from what is familiar and dear to them. May they find comfort in your presence, and may they feel your nearness even when they are far from home.

We also pray that you would bring people into their lives who will support and encourage them, and who will be a source of comfort and friendship. May they not feel alone, but rather be surrounded by a sense of belonging and purpose.

We ask these things in your holy name, Amen.

89. Prayer For Those With Dangerous Jobs

Dear God,

We lift up to you all those who have dangerous jobs. We recognize the bravery and dedication it takes to do work that puts their lives at risk, and we ask that you would be with them every step of the way.

We pray that you would keep them safe as they carry out their duties, and that you would protect them from harm. May they have the skills, knowledge, and equipment they need to do their jobs well, and may they always be aware of the potential dangers around them.

We also pray for their families, who may worry for their safety. May you give them peace and comfort, and may they trust in your care for their loved ones.

We thank you for those who serve and protect us in these important, but often dangerous, roles. We ask these things in your holy name, Amen.

90. A Prayer For The Isolated

Dear God,

We lift up to you all those who are feeling isolated today. We recognize that loneliness can be a difficult and overwhelming feeling, and we ask that you would be with those who are struggling with it.

We pray that you would bring people into their lives who will offer love, support, and companionship. May they find connection and belonging in the communities they are a part of, and may they know that they are not alone.

We also pray that you would give them the strength and resilience they need to face the challenges of isolation. May they find hope in your presence and find joy in the simple things.

We ask these things in your holy name, Amen.

91. A Prayer For The Disabled

Dear God,

We lift up to you all those who are living with disability. We recognize that life can present unique challenges for those with physical, mental, or emotional limitations, and we ask that you would be with them every step of the way.

We pray that you would give them the strength and courage they need to face the challenges they encounter, and that you would help them to find joy and purpose in their lives. May they find support and acceptance in the communities they are a part of, and may they know that they are not alone.

We also pray that you would give them the resources and assistance they need to live their lives to the fullest. May they have access to the medical care, education, and support they need to thrive.

We ask these things in your holy name, Amen.

92. A Prayer For the Unborn

Dear God,

We lift up to you all the unborn children in the world today. We recognize that every life is a precious gift from you, and we ask that you would watch over and protect these little ones as they grow in their mothers' wombs.

We pray that you would give them the strength and vitality they need to develop and grow, and that you would keep them safe from harm. May their mothers be blessed with good health and the support they need to care for their children, and may they feel your love and care for them.

We pray that you would guide and direct the steps of those who are considering abortion, and that you would give them the wisdom and strength to choose life for their unborn children. May they know that they are not alone, and that there is help and support available to them.

We ask these things in your holy name, Amen.

93. A Prayer For Broken Families

Dear God,

We recognize that family is an important source of love, support, and belonging, and we know that it can be a difficult and painful experience when those bonds are broken.

We pray that you would bring healing and restoration to these families. May they find your love and grace in the midst of their pain, and may they experience your peace and comfort.

We pray that you would give them the strength and courage they need to navigate the challenges they are facing, and that you would help them to find ways to move forward and rebuild their relationships. May they know that they are not alone, and that you are with them every step of the way.

We ask these things in your holy name, Amen.

94. A Prayer For the Dying

Dear God,

We lift up to you all those who are facing the end of their lives. We recognize that this can be a difficult and overwhelming time, and we ask that you would be with them as they navigate this journey.

We pray that you would give them the strength and comfort they need to face their mortality, and that you would ease their pain and suffering. May they find peace and acceptance in their final days, and may they feel your love and presence with them.

We also pray for their families and loved ones, who may be struggling with grief and loss. May they find comfort and support in each other, and may they feel your nearness and care for them.

We ask these things in your holy name, Amen.

95. A Prayer For the Displaced

Dear God,

We lift up to you all those who are displaced from their homes. Whether they are fleeing conflict, persecution, or natural disasters, we recognize that this can be a difficult and uncertain time for them.

We pray that you would give them the strength and resilience they need to face the challenges they are facing. May they find shelter, safety, and the resources they need to survive. May they also find support and compassion from those around them, and may they know that they are not alone.

We pray that you would bring about a resolution to the circumstances that have caused their displacement, and that they would be able to return to their homes and rebuild their lives. May they find hope and a sense of belonging in their new communities, and may they experience your love and care for them.

We ask these things in your holy name, Amen.

96. A Prayer For Immigrants

Dear God,

We lift up to you all the immigrants in the world today. We recognize that they may be facing challenges and uncertainties as they navigate life in a new country and culture.

We pray that you would give them the strength and courage they need to face these challenges, and that you would provide for their needs. May they find support and acceptance in the communities they are a part of, and may they know that they are not alone.

We also pray for those who are seeking asylum and refuge, that you would provide a safe and welcoming place for them to call home. May they find hope and a sense of belonging in their new home, and may they experience your love and care for them.

We ask these things in your holy name, Amen.

97. A Prayer For the Children

Dear God,

We lift up to you all the children in the world today. We recognize that they are the future of our world, and we ask that you would bless and protect them.

We pray that you would give them the opportunity to grow and thrive, and that you would provide for their needs. May they have access to education, medical care, and the resources they need to reach their full potential.

We also pray that you would protect them from harm and keep them safe from danger. May they be surrounded by love and care, and may they experience your presence and love every day.

We ask these things in your holy name, Amen.

98. A Prayer For the Desperate

Dear God,

We lift up to you all those who are feeling desperate and in need of hope. We recognize that life can present challenges and setbacks that can leave us feeling lost and unsure of the future.

We pray that you would open doors of opportunity for those who are struggling. May they find the resources and support they need to overcome their challenges, and may they have the courage and determination to pursue their dreams.

We pray that you would bring people into their lives who will encourage and support them, and who will be a source of hope and inspiration. May they find joy and purpose in their lives, and may they experience your love and care for them.

We ask these things in your holy name, Amen.

99. A Prayer For the Corrupt

Dear God,

We lift up to you all those who are living in corruption and wrongdoing. We recognize that this can be a destructive and harmful force in the world, and we ask that you would bring about change and righteousness.

We pray that you would expose the corruption and wrongdoing, and that you would bring those who are responsible to account. May justice be served, and may righteousness and truth prevail. We also pray that you would help them find your love, grace and mercy.

We also pray for those who have been affected by corruption and wrongdoing. May they find healing and restoration, and may they experience your love and care for them.

We ask these things in your holy name, Amen.

100. A Prayer For The Lord's Light

Dear God,

We lift up to you all those who are living in corruption and wrongdoing. We recognize that this can be a destructive and harmful force in the world, and we ask that you would bring about change and righteousness.

We pray that you would expose the corruption and wrongdoing, and that you would bring those who are responsible to account. May justice be served, and may righteousness and truth prevail.

We also pray for those who have been affected by corruption and wrongdoing. May they find healing and restoration, and may they experience your love and care for them.

We ask these things in your holy name, Amen.

www.ingramcontent.com/pod-product-compliance
Lightning Source LLC
Chambersburg PA
CBHW032041040426
42449CB00007B/977